ISBN 978-0-332-62884-4
PIBN 11249111

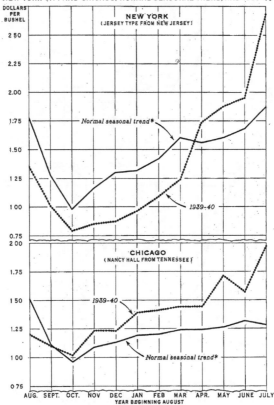

SWEETPOTATOES UNWEIGHTED AVERAGE WHOLESALE PRICES AT NEW YORK CITY AND CHICAGO, NORMAL SEASONAL TREND, AND 1939-40

ARITHMETIC AVERAGE OF THE 10 MIDDLE PRICES FOR EACH MONTH DURING THE 14-YEAR PERIOD 1925-39

U S DEPARTMENT OF AGRICULTURE   NEG 38569   BUREAU OF AGRICULTURAL ECONOMICS

ONIONS, YELLOW VARIETIES, U S NO 1 WHOLESALE PRICES AT NEW YORK
AND CHICAGO, NORMAL SEASONAL TREND, AND 1939 TO DATE

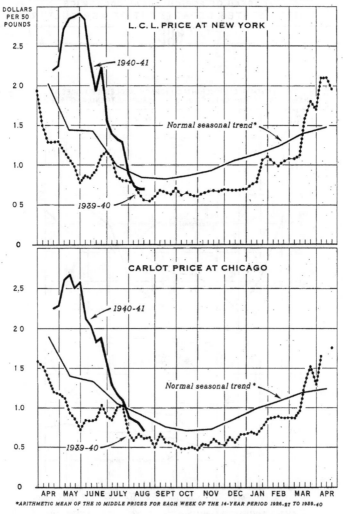

*ARITHMETIC MEAN OF THE 10 MIDDLE PRICES FOR EACH WEEK OF THE 14-YEAR PERIOD 1926-27 TO 1939-40

U. S. DEPARTMENT OF AGRICULTURE   NEG 38367   BUREAU OF AGRICULTURAL ECONOMICS

FIGURE 1

T H E   V E G E T A B L E   S I T U A T I O N

Summary

Continued heavy marketings of intermediate potatoes and market garden truck crops forced market prices downward during August. This price trend is more or less normal for this period of the year, however, and can be expected to be reversed as soon as the marketings from these areas are completed.

The late potato crop this season, totaling 290 million bushels, is indicated to be only slightly larger than the moderate sized crop of 1939; a small increase in the prospect for the 8 Eastern late States is about offset by a small decrease in the 12 Western late States. The late crop in the 10 Central States is indicated to be about the same as in 1939. Marketings of some of the earlier maturing late varieties are now moving, but the bulk of the late crop movement will not start before September.

The United States sweetpotato crop is indicated to total 65.7 million bushels, or about 7 million bushels less than in 1939. Prospects are reduced in all the important regions. As a result of the reduced crop prospect, early season market prices have averaged well above those of last season.

There was some improvement in the crop prospect for dry edible beans during July, and the forecast as of August 1 is for a crop of 14.6 million bags. This is 500,000 bags more than was indicated as of July 1 and 700,000 bags more than the production of 1939. Offsetting the increased crop is a probable reduction in the carry-over of perhaps 1 million bags from the record large carry-over last season.

Market supplies of truck crops for market during the remainder of the year are indicated to be about as large as those of last season. The late onion crop is reduced sharply below that of 1939, while the late production of cantaloupes, lettuce, and tomatoes is only slightly down. Production of

most other late truck crops is expected to be larger than that of a year

earlier. Indicated production of truck crops for processing showed little

change during the last month, and continues to be larger than in 1939.

                                                       - August 29, 1940

POTATOES

Marketings of the commercial portion of the intermediate potato
crop are declining, with most of the movement during recent weeks going by
motor truck. Shipments of early-maturing varieties in some of the late
States are increasing, however, and will continue to increase during the
next few months. Market prices of most varieties declined during recent
weeks as a result of the heavy marketings from the intermediate States, and
in late August averaged somewhat below those of a year earlier. Only
prices of Idaho Russet Burbanks averaged higher than in late August 1939.

The total intermediate potato crop was relatively large this season.
It totals 35.4 million bushels, or nearly 8 million bushels more than the
1939 crop. The commercial portion, indicated at 19.5 million bushels, is
about 4.6 million bushels larger than that of last season while the non-
commercial crop, indicated at 15.8 million, is 3.1 million bushels larger.
Most of the increase this season in the commercial crop occurred in Maryland,
Virginia, and New Jersey, where yields have been exceptionally high. There
was a slight increase in plantings in New Jersey. This large output has
resulted in rather heavy summer marketings and a greater-than-seasonal
decline in prices. The Surplus Marketing Administration has been buying
some potatoes for relief distribution during recent weeks.

The late crop is indicated to total 290 million bushels, about the
same as that of last year. An increase in prospective production in the
eight Eastern States is about offset by a decrease in the 12 Western States.
In the 10 Central late States the potato crop is indicated to be about the
same as in 1939. If the late crop is no larger than now indicated, it is
probable that there will be considerable improvement in the market situation
as soon as the effects of the large intermediate supply are eliminated. Last
season's late potato prices held to moderate levels as a result of moderate
supplies and purchasing power. Consumer purchasing power this season is
expected to average somewhat higher than in the previous season.

SWEETPOTATOES

Crop prospects declined during July as a result of unfavorable growing
conditions in some of the Southern States. Indicated production as of
August 1 totals 65.7 million bushels, or 3.1 million less than that of a month
earlier and about 7 million bushels less than the harvest of 1939. A smaller
than average crop of sweetpotatoes is indicated for each of the three important regions - the four Central Atlantic, the four Lower Atlantic, and the
eight South Central States. In the five North Central States, the crop is

slightly above that of 1939 but about average, while in California production is expected to be relatively large.

Because of a scarcity of old-crop sweetpotatoes market prices rose sharply in July and the early varieties of the new-crop opened at relatively high levels. In recent weeks, however, market prices declined seasonally as marketings increased. But in late August they averaged somewhat higher than a year earlier. The normal seasonal trend of prices of the important varieties is downward from the opening levels to a low in October and then upward during the remainder of the marketing season.

DRY BEANS

There was some improvement in the yield prospect for dry beans during July, with the total crop forecast rising to 14.6 million bags as of August 1. This represents an increase of about 500,000 bags during the month and 700,000 bags over the harvest of 1939. Above-average yields are indicated this season for all States except Maine, New York, and New Mexico.

Exports of 1939 crop beans continued heavy during June, and the total exported during the first 10 months of the season was 745,000 bags. In the corresponding period a year earlier exports amounted to only 241,000 bags. Much of the increased foreign trade this season is attributed to factors indirectly connected with the war in Europe, in that certain countries have been cut off from their normal sources of supply. Also a short bean crop in Chile has resulted in decreased competition from that country in the Latin American countries.

With exports for the season likely to total 850,000 bags and with domestic disappearance about as large as in the 1938 season, the carry-over into the 1940 season probably will be reduced considerably from the 3,000,000 bags carried over into the 1939 season. And with the new crop prospect at 14.6 million bags, the total supply probably will be close to 16.6 million bags compared with 17 million in 1939. August 1 stocks of California beans totaled 945,000 bags compared with 1,436,000 bags a year earlier. Also, June 1 stocks of Idaho beans totaled 917,000 bags compared with 979,000 on June 1, 1939.

TRUCK CROPS

Market supplies of truck crops for the remainder of the summer and most of the fall months will come largely from the late Northern States, where production prospects indicate supplies are about as large as in 1939. Most of the early and intermediate crops have been marketed except in New Jersey, which is still furnishing considerable quantities for eastern markets. Of the late truck crops only late onions show prospects of significantly smaller production than that of a year earlier. The reduction is 15 percent. Late cantaloupes and tomatoes are expected to be 3 percent smaller than in 1939 and late lettuce is down 2 percent. Other late truck crops are expected to be in somewhat larger supply than a year earlier, with late snap beans, domestic cabbage, cucumbers, and watermelons up sharply.

Although the seasonal trend of truck crop prices is slightly downward between July and August, prices of a few items rose slightly this season and the general level in late August was somewhat higher than a year earlier. Market prices of cabbage, cantaloupes, honeyballs, lettuce, spinach, and turnips, however, were definitely lower than a year ago. During the late fall months market supplies coming from the Northern States tend to decrease and prices rise seasonally.

The production of truck crops for fresh market produced largely in the early and intermediate States and marketed in the first half of 1940 exceeded that of the first half of 1939 by about 3 percent and was about 14 percent larger than the 10-year (1929-38) average. With late crops totaling about the same as a year earlier, the total volume of truck crops produced in 1940 probably will exceed that of 1939 and set a new high record. This increase is due to higher yields, since the acreage harvested probably will show a slight decrease.

Snap beans: Production in the first section of late States (Colorado, Michigan, New York, and Pennsylvania) is indicated to total 2.0 million bushels this season compared with 1.7 million a year earlier. This season's crop is more than double the 10-year (1928-39) average of 921,000 bushels. Supplementing this supply for immediate marketing, there are large quantities being produced in the market garden areas which usually move to market by motor truck. Also in late August the remainder of the intermediate crop was being marketed. In many areas in the Northern States dry weather is reported to have retarded the development of the crops. This is particularly true of the late planted fields. Except for short periods, market supplies of snap beans have been comparatively short this season, a situation which has resulted in somewhat higher prices than a year earlier. Market prices rose sharply during August, and in the latter part of the month averaged well above those of late August 1939.

Cabbage: Partly because of an increased acreage and partly because of favorable growing conditions, the late domestic cabbage crop is about one-third larger than that of 1939. It totals 396,800 tons and is about one-fifth larger than the 10-year (1928-39) average production. The crop is unusually large in the important producing States of Michigan, Wisconsin, New York, and Pennsylvania. Although a portion of this late crop is usually used for kraut manufacture, the supply this season is more than ample to meet this requirement and still provide a considerable fresh market surplus. The crop in the intermediate States is also larger than that of 1939. Because of this large supply, market prices during August averaged well below those of a year earlier. Early marketings from the late States are competing with the late marketings from the intermediate States, but the bulk of the late crop will not be ready for harvest until late September.

Cantaloupes: The late crop grown principally in Colorado, Michigan, and New Jersey is indicated to total 2,860,000 crates, or slightly less than in 1939. This crop follows relatively large second early and intermediate crops this season. In late August marketings from the North-eastern intermediate States were at a peak, but they are expected to decline after September 1. Supplies of honeydews and other miscellaneous melons are expected to be heavy in September. The large marketings in recent weeks caused market prices of cantaloupes, honeyballs, and Persian melons to decline to levels below those of late August 1939.

Cauliflower: The crop in the first section of late States (Colorado, New Jersey, New York, Utah, and Washington) is indicated to total 2,348,000 crates this season compared with 2,294,000 last season. Colorado is the leading source of carlot marketing, while the marketings from other States are moving by motor truck. Shipments from Colorado are limited by a marketing agreement to United States No. 1 grade, sizes 11 or 12, fairly uniform to uniform, and fairly tight to tight pack. In contrast with a slight decline in prices at Chicago during recent weeks, prices at New York have advanced sharply and in late August averaged substantially above those of a year earlier. The usual seasonal trend of prices is downward at this time of the year, reflecting increasing marketings from the late States.

Cucumbers: The first section of late States (Michigan and New York) has a production of cucumbers indicated at 513,000 bushels this season, compared with 372,000 bushels last season. Most of this production is located in New York State, where the marketing of the crop is in full progress. The market garden areas are also supplying considerable quantities, as is the intermediate area in New Jersey. Because of a temporary shortage in market supplies in recent weeks, however, market prices rose during August and in the latter part of the month averaged slightly higher than a year earlier.

Onions: Market prices of onions continued to decline in August as supplies increased to nearly normal levels. Prices were unusually high in late May because of the short early crop. There has been a rapid adjustment downward, however, and the averages in late August were at about normal levels, though somewhat higher than the relatively low prices in late August 1939. The normal trend of prices is sharply downward from April to September in eastern markets and from April to October in the Middle West. These prices usually rise gradually during the remainder of the marketing season.

For the 1940 season as a whole, onion supplies are relatively small. The early crop was cut short by dry weather, and now the western late crop is indicated to be 30 percent smaller than in 1939. The total late crop is about 15 percent smaller than a year earlier and totals only 11.9 million bags (100 pounds). In the Eastern States a production of 4.1 million bags is indicated for 1940 compared with 4.5 million in 1939. In the Central States the late crop is only slightly smaller, but in the far West the crop is reduced materially. It appears that the supply of sweet Spanish type onion, grown largely in the West, will be very short this season. A portion of the late crop is usually stored for late winter marketing.

Tomatoes: Production in the first section of late States (which includes most of the important truck-growing areas in the northern half of the country) is indicated to total 6.1 million bushels compared with 6.3 million bushels last season. This crop follows on the market a large

intermediate crop this season and competes directly with the peak of the
market garden output. Mid-August reports indicate that some late tomatoes
are now going to canneries because of low prices. Market prices usually
reach a seasonal low in August, when supplies are seasonally large, but
rise sharply during the remainder of the season. In late August this
year market prices averaged slightly higher than the unusually low level
of a year earlier.

      Watermelons: Production in the late States, indicated at 27.8 million
melons, is only slightly larger than that of a year earlier, but it follows
on the market a much larger second early crop, a part of which still remains
to be marketed. Most of the marketings from now to the end of the season
will be moved by motor truck. Although market prices declined seasonally
in recent weeks, in late August they averaged substantially higher than a
year earlier. The larger marketings this season at higher prices indicate
that demand for watermelons is much improved over that of last summer. A
part of this improvement in demand is attributed to the hot, dry weather
prevailing this summer and a part to increased consumer purchasing power.

TRUCK CROPS FOR PROCESSING

      There were only small changes indicated in the prospect for the
major truck crops for processing during August. The production forecast
for snap beans was increased slightly to 101,700 tons from 99,530 tons a
month ago and that of sweet corn to 668,000 tons from 642,800 tons in July.
The forecast for tomatoes was decreased from 1,906,300 to 1,860,900 tons.

      As compared with production in 1939, present prospects continue to
indicate considerable increases in the total pack of canned vegetables.
Since carry-over stocks are sharply below those of a year earlier, however,
the total supply probably will be only slightly larger than in the 1939
season.

Potatoes: Acreage, yield and production, average
1929-38, annual 1939 and indicated 1940

Group and classification	Acreage			Yield			Production		
	Average 1929-38	1939	For Harvest 1940	Average 1929-38	1939	Indicated 1940	Average 1929-38	1939	Indicated 1940
	1,000 acres	1,000 acres	1,000 acres	Bu.	Bu.	Bu.	1,000 bu.	1,000 bu.	1,000 bu.
Early									
Total ....:	421.0	450.3	461.5	87.9	103.2	106.0	37,205	46,473	48,899
Commercial .....:	169.4	193.2	194.6	122.9	148.1	152.5	20,812	28,611	29,669
Other ....:	251.6	257.1	266.9	65.2	69.5	72.0	16,393	17,862	19,230
Intermediate									
Total ....:	321.2	289.0	293.3	106.0	95.6	120.6	33,972	27,617	35,360
Commercial .....:	130.7	119.0	116.3	149.3	125.5	168.1	19,518	14,934	19,549
Other ....:	190.5	170.0	177.0	75.9	74.6	89.3	14,454	12,683	15,811
surplus late									
Total ....:	2,137.3	1,923.3	1,958.8	120.3	130.0	129.1	256,482	249,988	252,879
3 eastern ......:	611.0	568.0	583.0	161.7	154.0	163.2	98,875	87,487	95,145
5 central ......:	1,028.0	881.0	905.0	81.1	88.9	88.3	83,222	78,326	79,939
10 western ......:	498.2	474.3	470.8	150.1	177.5	165.2	74,384	84,175	77,795
other late									
Total ....:	416.2	364.1	373.8	94.6	109.7	99.5	39,291	39,938	37,176
5 eastern ......:	60.4	62.9	67.4	146.1	158.9	137.3	8,822	9,997	9,251
5 central ......:	348.0	293.0	298.0	86.1	99.8	91.3	29,862	29,241	27,193
2 western ......:	8.0	8.2	8.4	75.2	85.4	87.1	607	700	732
late ....:	2,553.5	2,287.4	2,332.6	116.1	126.7	124.3	295,772	289,926	290,055
late and intermediate ....:	2,874.7	2,576.4	2,625.9	115.0	123.3	123.9	329,744	317,543	325,415
United States total ....:	3,295.7	3,026.7	3,087.4	111.5	120.3	121.2	366,949	364,016	374,314
late									
8 eastern ......:	671.4	630.9	650.4	160.4	154.5	160.5	107,697	97,484	104,396
10 central ......:	1,376.0	1,174.0	1,203.0	82.2	91.6	89.1	113,084	107,567	107,132
12 western ......:	506.2	482.5	479.2	148.1	175.9	163.9	74,991	84,875	78,527

Compiled from reports of the Agricultural Marketing Service.

Potatoes: Acreage, yield per acre and production,
average 1929-38, annual 1939 and indicated 1940

Group and State	Acreage 10-year av. 1929-38	1939	1940	Yield per acre 10-year av. 1929-38	1939	Indi-cated 1940	Production 10-year av. 1929-38	1939	Indi-cated 1940
							1,000	1,000	1,00
	Acres	Acres	Acres	Bu.	Bu.	Bu.	bu.	bu.	bu.
Fall and winter 1/									
Florida, south	6,700	11,300	11,200	111	140	90	797	1,582	1,00
Texas	2,700	2,700	2,600	48	40	45	121	108	11
Total	9,400	14,000	13,800	98	121	82	918	1,690	1,12
Early (1)									
Florida, north ...	18,800	15,400	14,400	108	107	208	2,037	1,653	2,99
Hastings	16,100	13,000	12,000	110	105	220	1,736	1,365	2,64
La Crosse	2,100	1,600	1,600	113	130	170	231	208	27
West	600	800	800	108	100	100	70	80	8
Texas Lower Valley	9,200	5,200	7,900	87	80	90	785	416	71
Total	28,000	20,600	22,300	101	100	166	2,822	2,069	3,70
Early (2)									
Alabama	13,200	24,300	26,700	120	140	110	1,634	3,402	2,93
California	17,900	33,300	36,500	230	333	300	4,436	11,089	10,95
Georgia	1,600	2,300	3,800	140	160	150	225	368	57
Louisiana	22,900	24,000	22,000	73	60	68	1,691	1,440	1,49
Mississippi	2,300	3,500	3,000	92	80	60	208	280	18
South Carolina ...	12,400	13,500	14,000	148	150	150	1,862	2,025	2,10
Texas, other	12,900	9,200	8,600	66	65	70	854	600	59
Total	83,200	110,100	114,600	131	174	164	10,910	19,204	18,83
Second early									
Arkansas	5,000	4,600	4,100	88	85	100	436	391	41
North Carolina ...	32,700	36,000	32,400	142	125	150	4,680	4,500	4,86
Oklahoma	8,900	5,600	5,660	96	90	100	867	504	50
Tennessee	2,200	2,300	2,400	83	110	100	179	253	24
Total	48,800	48,500	43,900	126	116	137	6,162	5,648	6,01
Intermediate (1)									
Kansas	13,500	12,600	10,100	128	120	150	1,730	1,512	1,51
Kaw Valley	12,700	12,100	9,600	124	120	150	1,598	1,452	1,44
Scott County	800	500	500	166	120	150	132	60	7
Kentucky	4,800	3,100	3,100	99	153	120	446	474	37
Maryland	7,500	6,100	5,800	149	95	150	1,099	580	87
Missouri	5,800	5,700	5,400	136	200	225	768	1,140	1,21
Virginia	60,600	45,800	42,900	144	105	163	8,701	4,830	7,00
Norfolk district.	10,500	9,500	9,500	145	125	200	1,527	1,188	1,90
Eastern Shore ...	46,900	33,900	31,200	143	100	154	6,761	3,390	4,80
Other	3,200	2,400	2,200	129	105	135	413	252	29
Total	92,200	73,300	67,300	138	116	163	12,744	8,536	10,97
Intermediate (2)									
Nebraska	2,000	3,900	4,800	220	225	225	440	878	1,08
New Jersey	38,500	45,700	49,000	175	140	175	6,774	6,398	8,57
Total	40,500	49,600	53,800	178	147	179	7,214	7,276	9,65
All States	302,100	316,100	315,700	135	141	159	40,770	44,423	50,29

Compiled from reports of the Agricultural Marketing Service.
1/ Fall and winter crop States supply earliest new crop movement, starting in fall preceding year shown.

Potatoes and sweetpotatoes: Unweighted prices for stock of generally
good quality and condition (U. S. No. 1 when quoted) at shipping
points and terminal markets, week ended August 24, 1940
with comparisons

Market and variety	Week ended					
	1939	1940				
	Aug.	July	August			
	26	27	3	10	17	24
	Dol.	Dol.	Dol.	Dol.	Dol.	Dol.
Potatoes per 100 pounds						
F.o.b. shipping point						
Northern and Central						
New Jersey points ....:	1.10	.95	.92	.90	.83	.87
Terminal markets:						
New York City						
Cobblers, Virginia ....:	1.19	.97	.95	.91	.81	---
" , Long Island ....:	1.20	.94	.93	.91	.87	.90
" , New Jersey ....:	1.19	.93	.92	.88	.87	.91
" , Eastern ....:	1.20	.96	1.02	.91	.85	.91
Long Whites, Idaho ....:	---	3.11	2.66	---	2.27	2.48
" " , Washington .....:	2.46	---	2.77	2.71	2.62	2.50
Chippewas, Long Island ......:	1.29	---	1.00	.94	.91	.96
Russet Burbanks, Idaho ......:	2.47	---	2.65	2.66	2.70	2.64
Chicago						
Cobblers, Nebraska ....:	1.27	1.24	1.28	1.36	1.33	1.34
Bliss Triumphs, Nebraska ....:	1.50	---	1.65	1.85	1.58	1.54
" " , Oregon ......:	---	1.46	1.53	1.78	1.76	1.60
" " , Idaho ....:	1.78	1.48	1.53	1.84	1.67	1.55
Russet Burbanks, Idaho ......:	1.84	2.17	1.92	2.26	2.17	2.18
Excluding western stock .....:	1.16	1.12	1.20	1.29	1.26	1.17
Sweetpotatoes per bushel						
(new crop)						
New York						
Puerto Ricans,N.& S.Carolina :	1.12		2.69	2.65	2.46	2.25
Jerseys, Florida ....:	---	2.50	1.98	1.66	---	---
" ,N. & S. Carolina ....:	.74 1/	2.25	1.92	2.35	2.09	1.64
" , Maryland ....:	.90	---	---	---	1.97	1.88
Goldens, Maryland ....:	1.15	---	---	---	2.04	1.88
" , N. & S. Carolina ...:	.82	---	---	---	1.91	1.64
All varieties ....:	1.09	2.50	2.06	2.31	2.12	1.92
Chicago						
Triumph, Alabama ....:	---	2.49	2.04	1.68	1.98	1.65
Nancy Halls, Tennessee ......:	1.06	---	---	2.15	1.99	1.80
All varieties ....:	1.22	2.49	2.25	2.20	2.02	1.94

Compiled from reports of Agricultural Marketing Service.
1/ Average for 1 day.

Beans, dry edible: Acreage, yield and production by groups of States,
average 1929-38, annual 1939 and indicated 1940

Group of States	Acreage			Yield per acre			Production 1/		
	Average 1929-38	1939	For harvest 1940	Average 1929-38	1939	Indi- cated 1940	Average 1929-38	1939	Indi cate 1940
	1,000 acres	1,000 acres	1,000 acres	Pounds	Pounds	Pounds	1,000 bags	1,000 bags	1,00 bags
Me., Vt., N.Y., Mich., Wis., and Minn. 2/	723	610	688	714.0	949.2	779.9	5,162	5,790	5,36
Nebr., Mont., Idaho, Wyo. and Oreg. 3/	200	187	218	1,157.5	1,278.1	1,296.8	2,315	2,390	2,82
Kans., Colo., N. Mex., and Ariz. 4/	489	428	487	353.8	418.7	361.4	1,730	1,792	1,76
Calif. 5/	326	329	358	1,187.0	1,213.0	1,312.0	3,879	3,990	4,69
Total United States	1,737	1,554	1,751	759.0	898.5	836.5	13,086	13,962	14,64

Compiled from reports of Agricultural Marketing Service.
1/ Bags of 100 pounds; includes beans for seed. 2/ Largely pea beans, but most important source of Red Kidney, Yelloweye, and Cranberry. 3/ Largely Great Northern but Idaho most important source of supply of Small Reds. 4/ Largely Pinto. 5/ Miscellaneous varieties, mostly Lima, Baby Lima, Blackeye, Small White and Pink.

Sweetpotatoes: Acreage, yield and production by groups of States, average
1929-38, annual 1939 and indicated 1940

Group of States	Acreage			Yield per acre			Production		
	Average 1929-38	1939	For harvest 1940	Average 1929-38	1939	Indi- cated 1940	Average 1929-38	1939	Indi cate 1940
	Acres	Acres	Acres	Bu.	Bu.	Bu.	1,000 bu.	1,000 bu.	1,00 bu.
4 Central Atlantic 1/	67	61	61	121.5	140.5	130.7	8,141	8,568	7,97
4 Lower Atlantic 2/	283	280	257	82.2	91.0	79.3	23,263	25,490	20,38
8 South Central 3/	470	483	439	79.4	72.4	76.0	37,340	34,963	33,36
5 North Central 4/	30	28	28	84.3	87.8	89.8	2,528	2,458	2,51
California	11	10	12	105.0	120.0	120.0	1,164	1,200	1,44
Total United States	860	862	797	84.6	84.3	82.4	72,436	72,679	65,67

Compiled from reports of Agricultural Marketing Service.
1/ New Jersey, Delaware, Maryland, and Virginia. 2/ North Carolina, South Carolina Georgia, and Florida. 3/ Kentucky, Tennessee, Alabama, Mississippi, Arkansas, Louisiana, Oklahoma, and Texas. 4/ Indiana, Illinois, Iowa, Missouri, and Kansas.

Beans, dry, edible: Average wholesale price per 100 pounds at New York
City, and f.o.b. quotations per 100 pounds at Colorado and Idaho,
shipping points, 1938-40

Period	Wholesale price New York City								F.o.b. quotations 1/			
	Marrow		Calif. lima		Pea		Red Kidney		Colo. points Pinto		Idaho points Great Northern	
	1938	1939	1938	1939	1938	1939	1938	1939	1938	1939	1938	1939
	Dol.	Dol.	Dol.	Dol.	Dol.	Dol.	Dol.	Dol.	Dol.	Dol.	Dol.	Dol.
Month												
Sept.	5.33	5.87	5.42	6.43	3.12	4.76	3.86	6.14	3.62	4.95	2.30	3.83
Oct.	5.11	5.02	5.34	6.35	2.90	3.84	4.17	5.32	3.82	4.18	2.23	3.28
Nov.	4.72	4.81	5.31	6.09	2.72	3.71	3.57	4.78	3.86	3.92	2.31	3.04
Dec.	4.47	4.63	5.27	5.97	2.66	3.77	3.29	4.86	4.06	4.04	2.30	2.90
	1939	1940	1939	1940	1939	1940	1939	1940	1939	1940	1939	1940
Jan.	4.61	4.56	5.25	5.82	2.75	3.98	3.38	5.04	4.25	3.94	2.25	3.20
Feb.	5.21	4.55	5.25	5.74	2.75	4.00	3.23	4.95	4.15	3.66	2.25	3.09
Mar.	5.32	4.55	5.14	5.55	2.75	3.86	3.10	4.75	4.18	3.48	2.20	2.94
Apr.	5.02	4.50	5.15	5.50	2.78	3.81	2.98	4.71	4.38	3.59	2.39	3.04
May	4.95	4.50	5.36	5.51	3.04	3.90	3.67	4.75	4.31	3.72	2.65	3.26
June	4.89	4.50	5.39	5.55	2.98	3.87	3.78	4.68	3.74	3.49	2.45	2.91
July	4.75	4.46	5.40	5.51	2.99	3.82	3.63	4.60	3.82	3.13	2.52	2.77
Week period												
July 6	4.85	2/ 4.50	5.40	2/ 5.55	2.90	2/ 3.82	3.70	2/ 4.60	3.80	----	2.45	----
13	4.85	4.46	5.40	5.55	2.90	3.82	3.70	4.60	3.78	3.25	----	2.82
20	4.68	4.45	5.40	5.55	2.97	3.82	3.53	4.60	3.82	3.30	2.48	2.82
27	4.65	4.45	5.40	5.45	3.15	3.82	3.57	4.60	3.90	3.20	2.62	2.72
Aug. 3	4.65	4.49	5.38	5.45	3.15	3.82	3.75	4.56	3.95	2.78	2.60	2.70
10	4.65	4.50	5.37	5.45	3.03	3.76	3.75	4.55	3.98	2.82	2.58	----
17	4.65	4.50	5.40	5.45	3.00	3.68	3.75	4.50	3.98	2.90	2.58	2.50

New York, compiled from The Producers Price Current, f.o.b. quotations from reports
of Agricultural Marketing Service.

1/ Prices are for Wednesday of week shown.
2/ Average for 1 day.

Beans, dry, edible: F.o.b. price per 100 pounds, rail, California, 1938-40

(price in Dol.)

Period	Bayo			Blackeye			Cranberry			Kidney			Lima (standard)			Lima (baby)			Pink			Red			White (small)		
	1938	1939	1940	1938	1939	1940	1938	1939	1940	1938	1939	1940	1938	1939	1940	1938	1939	1940	1938	1939	1940	1938	1939	1940	1938	1939	1940
Month																											
Sept.	6.06	4.91		2.95	4.74		4.75	4.31		4.35	5.56		4.68	5.44		3.31	4.07		3.77	4.87		3.33	4.40		2.93	4.82	
Oct.	5.27	6.47		2.98	4.62		4.34	3.50		4.33	5.41		4.48	5.50		3.14	3.54		3.62	4.67		3.37	3.98		2.98	4.20	
Nov.	4.91	6.75		3.04	4.39		4.01	3.25		4.81	5.38		4.42	5.13		2.88	3.30		3.56	4.51		3.16	3.41		2.86	3.81	
Dec.	4.75	5.75		3.20	4.44		4.28	3.11		4.60	5.83		4.45	4.81		2.84	3.28		3.34	4.47		3.04	3.29		2.84	3.81	
Jan.		6.75	4.78		3.21	4.59		3.32	4.56		6.22	4.46		4.83	3.34		2.85	3.46		3.46	4.50		2.85	3.33		2.85	3.91
Feb.		7.19	4.94		3.22	4.66		3.20	4.56		6.24	4.40		4.75	3.27		2.79	3.42		3.42	4.38		2.75	3.25		2.81	3.79
M.		7.25	5.00		3.12	4.56		3.12	4.55		5.51	4.38		4.72	3.25		2.72	3.29		3.29	4.30		2.75	3.60		2.77	3.76
Apr.		7.25	4.97		3.69	4.63		3.00	4.34		5.30	4.47		4.66	3.27		2.76	3.20		3.20	4.25		2.74	3.58		2.83	3.67
May		7.25	4.95		3.75	4.43		3.00	4.11		5.38	4.59		4.68	3.49		2.98	3.28		3.28	4.25		2.84	3.58		3.04	3.78
June		7.25	4.84		3.60	4.25		2.92	3.75		5.53	4.66		4.72	3.48		2.97	3.29		3.29	4.42		2.84	3.48		3.04	3.82
July		7.21	4.51		3.53	4.03		2.84	3.75		5.44	4.66		4.67	3.48		2.91	3.25		3.25	4.15		2.80	3.41		3.01	3.72
Week ended																											
July 10		7.25	3.75		3.58	4.78		4.05	2.92		5.55	4.68		4.68	2.92		2.92	3.50		3.25	4.28		2.50	3.42		3.02	3.78
17		7.25	3.75		3.50	4.68		4.00	2.85		5.42	4.70		4.65	2.92		2.92	3.50		3.25	4.12		2.50	3.40		2.98	3.75
24		7.25	3.75		3.50	4.35		3.92	2.80		5.42	4.65		4.65	2.90		2.90	3.48		3.24	4.12		2.50	3.40		3.00	3.70
31		7.10	3.75		3.50	4.25		3.82	2.80		5.38	4.62		4.62	2.90		2.90	3.42		3.24	4.06		2.50	3.40		3.05	3.68
Aug. 7		7.10	3.75		3.50	4.10		3.70	2.80		5.25	4.65		4.65	2.90		2.90	3.40		3.26	4.04		2.80	3.40		3.05	3.68
14		7.10	3.75		3.40	3.85		3.60	2.72		5.12	4.65		4.65	2.90		2.90	3.40		3.26	3.90		2.85	3.40		3.02	3.68
21		7.10	3.65		3.48	3.50		3.50	2.72		4.88	4.62		4.62	2.90		2.90	3.38		3.22	3.80		2.85	3.40		3.02	3.60

Compiled as follows:
September 1938 to February 1940 from Federal State Market News Service, "Bulletin No. 315", Sacramento; beginning March 1940 from "Bean Market Review", weekly, San Francisco.

Truck crops: Commercial acreage and production for market,
average 1929-38, annual 1939 and indicated 1940

Crop and seasonal group	Acreage			Unit	Production		
	10-year average 1929-38	1939	Prelimi-nary 1940		10-year average 1929-38	1939	Indica-ted 1940
	Acres	Acres	Acres				
tichokes ....:	8,350	10,200	10,550:	boxes:	875	1,122	---
paragus 1/,total U.S.:	106,990	123,290	129,270:	1000crt:	9,786	10,875	11,920
ma beans, total U.S. :	11,460	13,750	---:	" bu.:	714	1,100	---
all through inter- :							
mediate (1) ....:	6,710	8,500	8,100:	" " :	416	720	517
Intermediate (2) .....:	5,240	4,600	4,550:	" " :	357	351	354
nap beans, total U.S. :	144,170	177,190	---:	" " :	12,076	16,580	---
Fall through inter- :							
mediate (1) ....:	106,390	126,350	111,350:	" " :	8,308	11,343	8,995
Intermediate (2) .....:	12,150	11,500	10,700:	" " :	1,171	911	941
" (3) .....:	---	7,350	7,200:	" " :	---	757	649
Late (1) ....:	6,950	13,050	13,700:	" " :	921	1,682	2,006
eets, total U.S. .....:	10,940	11,640	---:	" " :	1,942	2,021	---
Early and second early:	8,160	8,270	6,600:	" " :	1,162	1,122	890
Intermediate ....:	2,450	2,820	2,900:	" " :	663	690	731
abbage 1/, total U.S. :	170,970	182,220	187,230:	ton	1,154,400	1,137,200	---
Fall through second :							
early ....:	61,650	74,930	75,430:	"	329,600	379,200	381,000
Intermediate ....:	31,900	35,490	36,400:	"	185,500	219,700	228,400
Late :							
Domestic ....:	41,030	40,300	43,000:	"	326,500	297,900	396,800
Danish ....:	36,390	31,500	32,400:	"	292,800	240,400	---
antaloupes, total U.S.:	118,210	133,410	129,060:	1000crt:	14,890	14,402	14,237
Early and second early:	77,160	85,040	83,180:	" " :	10,171	9,105	8,966
Intermediate ....:	21,420	25,450	22,250:	" " :	2,109	2,358	2,411
Late ....:	19,630	22,920	23,630:	" " :	2,610	2,939	2,860
arrots 1/, total U.S. :	35,080	43,520	---:	" bu.:	12,560	16,061	---
Fall through second :							
early ....:	27,180	34,100	35,950:	" " :	9,279	12,686	13,928
Intermediate ....:	1,680	2,170	2,500:	" " :	466	514	616
auliflower, total U.S.:	29,140	28,450	---:	" crt:	7,284	8,476	---
Fall, winter and early:	17,300	15,450	16,610:	" " :	4,639	4,832	4,841
Late (1) ....:	7,860	8,500	9,050:	" " :	1,733	2,294	2,348
elery, total U.S. ....:	35,040	40,240	---:	" " :	9,525	11,527	---
Fall through second :							
early ....:	17,540	20,800	21,300:	" " :	4,770	6,003	7,052
Intermediate ....:	4,130	4,640	4,680:	" " :	1,066	1,370	1,191
Late (1) ....:	11,710	12,700	13,960:	" " :	3,193	3,543	---
orn, sweet (N. J.) ...:	24,350	26,000	25,000:	" ears:	116,020	114,400	140,000
ucumbers, total U.S. .:	45,200	43,410	---:	" bu.:	4,171	4,656	---
Fall through second :							
early ....:	33,100	29,950	28,550:	" " :	2,740	3,036	2,673
Intermediate ....:	8,320	8,100	8,200:	" " :	1,048	1,085	1,062
Late (1) ....:	2,520	3,560	3,870:	" " :	290	372	513

Continued -

Truck crops: Commercial acreage and production for market,
average 1929-38, annual 1939 and indicated 1940 - Continued

Crop and seasonal group	Acreage			Unit	Production		
	10-year average 1929-38	1939	Prelimi-nary 1940		10-year average 1929-38	1939	Indic tec 1940
	Acres	Acres	Acres				
Eggplant, total U.S. ..:	3,710	4,500	3,650:	1000bu.	822	1,092	6
Fall through second :							
early ....:	2,620	3,300	2,450:	"	531	816	
Late ....:	1,090	1,200	1,200:	"	291	276	
Kale (Va.) ....:	1,700	1,100	1,100:	"	598	550	
Lettuce, total U. S. ..:	156,840	171,420	----:	1000crt	19,536	24,070	
Early and second early:	93,540	107,150	93,190:	" " :	10,574	14,155	14,0
Intermediate ....:	4,850	4,130	4,340:	" " :	948	801	9
Late ....:	26,060	27,590	28,580:	" " :	3,622	4,210	4,1
Onions, total U. S. ...:	121,980	131,140	108,270:	1000 :	14,157	17,840	14,8
Early and intermediate:				sacks:			
(1) ....:	62,130	66,200	46,450:	:	3,005	3,246	2,8
Intermediate (2) .....:	6,440	6,190	6,050:	" :	862	630	7
Late ....:	53,410	58,750	55,770:	" :	10,290	13,964	11,8
Green peas, total U.S. :	101,830	105,650	----:	1000bu.:	7,690	9,627	-
Early through :							
intermediate (2) ....:	61,660	66,190	55,440:	" " :	4,044	5,163	4,0
Late (1) ....:	19,380	22,910	23,700:	" " :	1,979	2,671	2,4
Late (2) ....:	3,210	5,100	6,700:	" " :	309	527	5
Green peppers,total U.S:	18,020	21,930	---:	" " :	4,068	5,066	-
Fall through second :							
early ....:	9,730	10,830	9,960:	" " :	2,072	2,609	1,7
Intermediate (1) .....:	950	2,000	1,900:	" " :	164	280	3
" (2) .....:	5,940	6,700	6,900:	" " :	1,445	1,541	1,7
Shallots (La.) ......:	---	5,400	5,000:	" " :	---	674	6
Spinach, total U. S. ..:	59,430	61,030	---:	" " :	12,603	13,430	-
Fall through second :							
early ....:	51,620	52,290	53,130:	" " :	10,633	10,943	10,5
Intermediate ....:	840	1,400	1,600:	" " :	109	175	2
Tomatoes, total U. S. .:	177,260	210,550	203,420:	" " :	19,584	24,782	-
Fall through second :							
early ....:	91,850	119,100	110,500:	" " :	7,790	10,713	9,0
Intermediate ....:	43,810	48,050	51,580:	" " :	5,873	6,667	7,3
Late (1) ....:	33,700	36,100	36,240:	" " :	4,957	6,307	6,1
Late (2) ....:	7,900	7,300	5,100:	" " :	964	1,095	
Watermelons, total U.S.:	254,780	277,220	279,630:	1000 :	68,900	66,204	79,8
Early through second :				melons:			
early ....:	196,620	199,800	207,100:	" :	48,166	39,065	51,9
Late ....:	58,160	77,420	72,530:	" :	20,734	27,139	27,8
Total planted or indi- :							
cated to be planted as:							
of Aug. 15 ....:	1,545,470	1,733,730	1,677,390:	:			
Approximate acreage of :							
late crops as of :							
Aug. 15 ....:	353,350	394,900	394,430	:			

Compiled from reports of Agricultural Marketing Service .

Truck crops: Unweighted average wholesale price at New York and Chicago
for stock of generally good quality and condition (U. S. No. 1 when
quoted) for week ended August 24, 1940 with comparisons

Market and commodity	Unit	Week ended					
		1939 Aug.	1940 July	Aug.			
		26	27	3	10	17	24
New York		Dol.	Dol.	Dol.	Dol.	Dol.	Dol.
ans, fava, N. Y. ....:	Bushel	----	----	1.25	1.38	1/1.50	----
" lima, L. Is. ....:	"	.74	1.50	1.38	1.75	1.52	2.08
" " Pa. ....:	"	1/ .62	----	1.50	1.97	1.69	----
" " N. J. ....:	"	.66	1.27	1.19	1.78	1.58	1.88
" snap, green, N. Y. .:	"	1.01	1.29	1.10	1.72	1.83	1.80
" " wax, N. Y. ...:	"	1.17	1.54	1.55	1.82	1.70	1.94
" " " eastern .:	"	1.15	1.52	1.55	1.81	1.70	1.79
ets, bunched, Pa. ....:	Crate	.74	.35	.36	----	----	----
" topped, N. J. ....:	Bushel	.64	.51	.64	.61	.53	.53
cccoli, Calif. 2/ ....:	Pony crate	2.60	3.00	2.94	3.04	2.85	3.25
" eastern ....:Crt. 1doz.bunches:		1.23	----	1.29	.83	.77	.91
.bbage, Pa. ....:1-1/2 bu. hamper :		.95	.43	.65	.68	.55	.68
" N. Y. ....:	50 lb. sack	.90	----	.48	.52	.55	.55
" nearby ....:1-1/2 bu. hamper :		----	.40	.64	.74	.72	.75
ntaloups, Calif. ....:	Jumbos 36's	3.71	4.38	3.64	2.94	3.08	3.79
" Utah ....:	Jumbos 36's and Standard 45's	4.25	----	----	3.06	2.84	3.64
" Md. and Dela. ...:	2/3 crate	.96	----	.99	.91	1.09	1.44
irrots, topped, washed,N.Y.:	Bushel	.65	.84	.75	.73	.73	.72
" " " Pa.:	"	.54	.86	.48	.50	.56	.62
" bunched, Calif. ..:	L. A. crate	2.62	4.29	3.38	3.31	3.77	3.68
iuliflower, Colo. ....:	Pony crate	1.25	----	----	1.88	1.78	1.58
" N. Y. and L.Is:	" "	.99	1.54	1.54	2.31	2.62	----
ilery, N. Y. and N. J. ...:	1/2 crate	.62	.93	.92	.91	1.07	.78
" N. Y. ....:	2/3 crate	.80	1.16	1.18	1.15	1.25	.99
ilery cabbage, N. Y. .....:	Eastern lettuce crate	.62	----	.65	.66	1/.62	.69
" " Ohio ......:	16 qt. basket	----	----	.40	.41	.49	.70
irn, green, N. J. ....:	Bushel	----	.56	.54	.71	.74	.78
" " N. Y. ....:	"	.56	----	.68	.75	.78	.87
icumbers, L. Is. ....:	"	1.12	----	1.25	1.50	1.16	1.12
" N. J. ....:	"	1.06	.95	1.50	1.79	1.19	1.06
" Md. and Dela. ..:	"	----	.98	1.60	1.69	.98	.94
gplant, N. C. ....:	"	----	1.22	1.00	.84	.69	----
" Va. ....:	"	----	1.45	.91	.85	.62	----
" N. J. ....:	"	.33	1.55	1.28	1.20	.66	.56
.dive, Ohio ....:	16 qt. basket	.50	----	----	.49	.48	.40
ineyball, Calif. ....:	Jumbos 36's and Standard 45's	3.33	2.73	3.12	3.35	2.85	2.92
ineydews, Calif. ....:	Crt. 9's - 12's:	1.99	1.58	2.25	1.88	2.24	2.10
" Ariz. ....:	"	1.76	2.03	1.74	1.79	2.16	2.03
ittuce, iceberg, Calif. ..:	L. A. crate	4.31	2.90	3.64	2.77	2.71	2.86
" " N. Y. ...:	2 doz. crate	.78	.76	.96	.83	.54	----
" Big Boston ....:	"	.92	.51	.78	.80	.66	.56

Continued-

Truck crops; Unweighted average wholesale price at New York and Chicago
for stock of generally good quality and condition (U. S. No. 1 when
quoted) for week ended August 24, 1940 with comparisons - Continued

Market and commodity	Unit	1939 Aug. 26	1940 July 27	Aug. 3	Aug. 10	Aug. 17	Aug. 24
		Dol.	Dol.	Dol.	Dol.	Dol.	Dol.
New York - Continued							
Mushrooms, N. Y. and Pa. ..:	3 lb. basket	.68	.84	.84	.91	.79	.8!
Okra, N. C. ....:	1/2 bushel	1/ .45	1.13	.72	1.06	1.09	1.0(
" Fla. ....:	Bushel	----	1.62	1.17	1.72	1.62	1.5?
" N. J. ....:	12 qt. basket	.35	1.05	.78	.95	.95	1.0?
Onion, yellows, eastern ...:	50 lb. sack	.57	1.29	.92	.74	.70	.7(
" sweet Spanish ......:	"	1.27	----	----	----	----	2.0(
Parsley, N. J. ....:	Bushel	.60	.61	.51	.64	.57	1/.6?
" Pa. ....:	1/2 bushel	.30	.39	.36	.36	.45	.44
Peas, Colo. ....:	Bushel	1.58	1.99	1.55	1.54	1.71	1.99
" Idaho ....:	"	1.46	1.56	1.27	1.44	1.57	1.88
" N. Y. ....:	"	----	1.08	----	1/.82	1.00	1.1?
Peppers, sweet, N. C. .....:	"	----	.78	.56	.68	.52	.5?
" ". N. J. .....:	"	.35	.81	.59	.72	.52	.5?
" hot, N. J. ....:	"	.34	.75	.54	.65	.46	.4?
" " N. and S.Car.:	"	----	.44	.50	.50	.35	.4?
" red, N. J. ....:	"	.85	----	1.38	.96	.86	.9?
" " N. C. ....:	"	----	----	.88	.85	.52	----
Persian melons, Calif. ....:	Standard 6's	1.98	----	3.08	2.03	1.68	1.6?
Radishes, nearby ....:	Bushel	----	.61	1/.68	.77	.55	.6?
Rutabagas, N. J. ....:	"	----	.50	.48	.46	.46	.4?
Spinach, N. Y. ....:	"	1.23	.39	.77	1.08	1.07	.88
Squash, green, N. J. ......:	"	.38	.49	.47	.77	.52	.48
" white, N. J. ......:	"	.38	.56	.40	.55	.54	.4?
" yellow, N. J. .....:	"	.35	.51	.38	.61	.54	.4?
Tomatoes, Md. and Va. .....:	Lug	----	.60	.72	.68	.58	1/.4?
" Pa. ....:	"	.50	----	.82	.80	.69	.6(
" N. Y. ....:	"	.50	.82	.89	.77	.58	.5?
Turnips, nearby ....:	Bushel and crate	1.46	.60	.62	.54	.71	.61
Watermelons, Tom Watsons 28-30 lb. av. ....:	Bulk per car	----	291.	258.	262.	----	----
Watermelons, Thurman Gray 22-26 lb. av. ....:	"	3/135.	272.	285.	238.	1/235.	----
Chicago							
Beans, lima, Md. ....:	Bushel	----	2.52	2.04	2.00	----	----
" " Mich. ....:	12 qt. basket	.41	----	----	----	1.12	1.29
" snap, green, Ill. ..:	Bushel	.76	.86	1.48	1/1.38	1/2.25	1/2.62
" " " eastern:	"	.75	----	1.64	2.14	2.80	2.82
" " " N. Y. .:	"	----	----	1.81	2.21	3.06	2.88
" " wax, N. Y. ...:	"	----	----	1.38	1.88	2.41	2.88
" " " eastern .:	"	1.33	----	1.38	1.62	2.41	2.67
Beets, topped, Ill. ....:	"	.50	.48	.50	.40	.30	.28
Broccoli, Calif. 2/ ......:	Pony crate	2.46	----	2.25	2.25	2.25	2.62

Continued -

Truck crops: Unweighted average wholesale price at New York and Chicago
for stock of generally good quality and condition (U. S. No. 1 when
quoted) for week ended August 24, 1940 with comparisons - Continued

Market and commodity	Unit	1939 Aug. 26	1940 July 27	July 3	Aug 10	Aug 17	Aug 24
		Dol.	Dol.	Dol.	Dol.	Dol.	Dol.
ussel sprouts, Calif. ...:	1/2 drum	2.65	----	----	----	3.00	2.52
bage, Ill. ....:	Crts. 50-75 lb.:	1.02	.37	.40	.50	.48	.50
" Wis. ....:	"	.93	----	.42	1/.50	.47	.55
" red, Ill. ....:	Bushel	.45	.95	.62	.69	.56	.60
" " Mich. ....:	"	----	----	.91	.92	.78	.75
italoups, Calif. ....:	Jumbos 36's and Standard 45's	2.50	3.97	2.78	2.62	3.28	3.44
" N. Mex. ....:	"	2.18	----	2.68	2.42	2.50	1/2.88
" Colo. ....:	"	2.45	----	----	----	2.97	3.14
rrots, topped, Ill. .....:	Bushel	.50	1.37	1.08	.98	.88	.76
" bunched, Calif. ..:	L. A. crate	2.50	3.69	2.75	2.35	1/3.75	3.22
saba melons, Calif. ......:	Crt. 6's - 8's :	1.82	----	----	2.22	1.90	1.86
" " " ....:	Standard 6's-9's:	1.62	----	----	2.00	1.69	1.69
iliflower, Colo. ....:	Pony crate	1.38	----	1.32	1.38	1.30	1.16
lery, Mich. ....:	Flat crate	.41	.44	.47	.44	.41	.44
lery cabbage, Mich. .....:	Lug 10's - 12's	----	----	.60	.75	.75	.80
rn, green, Ill. ....:	Sack, 4 - 5 doz.:	.30	.59	.24	.30	.34	.32
jumbers, Mich. ....:	Bushel	.86	----	----	2.46	1.28	1.12
" Ill. ....:	"	.91	1.01	1.89	2.33	1.19	.96
ll, Ill. ....:	Bundle	----	----	.28	.24	.25	.20
gplant, Ill. ....:	Bushel	.40	----	----	1.69	1.79	1.21
" Mo. ....:	"	.40	----	----	1.50	1.69	1.25
ive, Ill. ....:	"	.58	.62	.45	.60	.66	.69
' Ohio ....:	24 qt. basket :	----	.52	.50	.44	.49	.46
carole, Ill. ....:	Bushel	.40	.39	.35	.44	.39	.40
eydews, Calif. ....:	Standard and Jumbos 6's - 12's:	1.56	----	----	1.79	1.90	1.88
" Ariz. ....:	"	1.48	1.69	1.62	1.70	1.68	----
tuce, Calif. ....:	L. A. crate	3.52	2.22	2.71	2.15	2.45	2.55
shrooms, Ill. ....:	Pound	.31	.31	.30	.30	.32	.32
stard, Ill. ....:	Bushel	.25	.25	.34	.44	.39	.43
ra, Tenn. ....:	"	.72	1.46	1.20	.99	.98	1.22
' Ill. ....:	"	.89	----	1/1.50	1.25	1.00	1.31
ions, yellows, Ill. .....:	50 lb. sack	.55	1.04	.88	.84	.81	.69
sley, Ill. ....:	Box	.22	.23	.28	.23	.24	.27
s, Idaho ....:	Bushel	1.50	1.55	1.24	1.39	1.54	1.70
' Colo. ....:	"	1.38	1.62	1.32	1.38	1.36	1.72
ppers, Ill. and Ind. ....:	"	.35	----	.78	1.05	.90	.64
' Tenn. ....:	"	----	.94	.68	.80	.71	.49
rsian melons, Calif. ....:	Crate - Std. 6's:	1.83	2.50	2.38	2.00	2.29	1.90
' " " ....:	Pony crts.6's-3's:	----	1.55	1.75	1.50	1.64	1.42
tabagas, Va. ....:	50 lb. sack :	.75	.96	.90	.90	.80	.80
inach, Colo. ....:	1/2 crate	1.38	----	1.45	1.32	1.73	1.78
" Mich. ....:	Bushel	.89	.41	.71	.75	.89	1.08

Continued -

Truck crops: Unweighted average wholesale price at New York and Chicago
for stock of generally good quality and condition (U. S. No. 1 when
quoted) for week ended August 24, 1940 with comparisons - Continued

Market and commodity	Unit	1939	Week ended 1940				
			July 27	Aug. 3	10	17	24
		Dol.	Dol.	Dol.	Dol.	Dol.	Dol.
Chicago - Continued							
Squash, white, Ill. ....:	Bushel	.24	.50	.48	1.01	.58	.48
" yellow, Ill. ......:	"	.24	.54	.50	.84	.56	.48
" acorn type, Ill. .:	"	.32	.82	.56	.90	.72	1.19
Tomatoes, Calif. ....:	Lug	----	----	1.25	1.37	1.40	1.25
" Tenn. ....:	"	----	.88	.92	.90	.68	1.00
Turnips, Ill. ....:	Bushel	1.00	.54	.44	.69	.85	.75
Watermelons, Cuban Queen ..:	Per melon						
	all sizes	.16	.39	.26	.27	.20	.25

Compiled from reports of the Agricultural Marketing Service.
1/ Average for 1 day.
2/ Heads and shoots.
3/ 26 - 28 lb. average.

Truck crops and potatoes: Carlot (rail and boat) shipments from
originating points in the United States for the week ended
August 24, 1940 with comparisons

Commodity	1939 Aug. 26	July 27	August 3	10	17	24
	Cars	Cars	Cars	Cars	Cars	Cars
Asparagus	--	--	--	--	1	1
Beans, snap and lima	4	15	19	16	8	2
Beets	2	---	---	1	---	
Broccoli	16	11	10	10	8	7
Cabbage	74	18	21	41	30	37
Cantaloups	305	638	364	233	216	398
Carrots	107	66	61	79	83	73
Casaba melons	3	---	---	---	1	---
Cauliflower	67	15	35	88	159	169
Celery	107	65	85	71	117	99
Corn	9	---	10	7	2	12
Cucumbers	61	15	6	2	12	11
Greens, except spinach	1	---	---	1	2	7
Honeyball melons	15	11	19	18	22	5
Honeydew "	160	308	171	145	133	147
Lettuce and romaine	813	1,103	1,138	848	888	883
Mixed melons	43	17	43	76	82	62
" vegetables	297	154	179	268	259	264
Onions	481	174	178	183	266	273
Peas	247	203	208	216	214	186
Peppers	---	4	---	1	---	---
Persian melons	5	2	7	7	31	43
Spinach	25	18	24	18	19	61
Sweet potatoes	144	74	56	44	30	81
Tomatoes	537	159	122	102	114	240
Turnips and rutabagas	4	3	---	5	3	5
Watermelons	225	3,189	1,137	854	750	426
Total	3,752	6,262	3,893	3,334	3,450	3,492
Potatoes, total	1,777	1,873	1,126	1,635	1,538	1,520
Early	8	275	85	8	8	2
Intermediate	296	700	369	300	200	210
Late	1,473	898	672	1,377	1,330	1,308
Total above	5,529	8,135	5,019	5,019	4,988	5,012
Relief						
Cabbage	---	---	---	43	44	50
Peas	27	---	30	30	2	---
Potatoes	---	189	98	203	215	198
Tomatoes	---	141	79	---	---	---

Compiled from reports of Agricultural Marketing Service.

Truck crops for processing: Commercial acreage and production,
annual 1938-40, and condition as of August 15, 1939 and 1940

Commodity	Planted acreage			Production			:1939:
	1938	1939	1940 1/	1938	1939	1940 1/	Pct.
	Acres	Acres	Acres	Tons	Tons	Tons	
Beans, lima ..:	55,010	50,540	50,670	28,730	28,650	---	81.6 7
Beans, snap ..:	76,010	54,860	57,590	128,400	94,150	101,700	---
Beets ....:	12,380	9,060	12,200	70,780	38,740	---	72.8 7
Cabbage for :							
kraut ....:	18,600	20,140	18,900	195,400	146,600	---	74.3 8
Corn, sweet ..:	361,170	254,460	328,710	882,800	661,100	668,000	---
Cucumbers for :							
pickles .....:	88,700	64,620	92,760	6,107	3,859	---	76.1 7
Peas, green ..:	334,920	260,070	323,980	302,540	198,110	289,010	
Pimentos .....:	26,390	22,090	15,490	38,840	23,190	---	75.5 5
Spinach 2/ ...:	17,470	13,660	12,400	30,400	36,500	36,910	
Tomatoes .....:	410,160	371,730	391,630	1,742,600	1,996,800	1,860,900	
Total ......:	1,400,810	1,121,430	1,304,330	3,416,597	3,227,699		

Compiled from reports of Agricultural Marketing Service.

1/ Preliminary.
2/ Harvested acreage in 1938 and 1939; planted acreage in 1940.

Vegetables, frozen: Cold storage holdings, August 1, 1940,
with comparisons

Commodity	1939		1940	
	July 1	August 1	July 1	August 1
	1,000 lb.	1,000 lb.	1,000 lb.	1,000 lb.
Asparagus ....:	7,499	6,472	7,438	7,138
Beans, lima ....:	8,562	8,087	8,300	8,388
Beans, snap ....:	4,199	6,312	3,781	5,309
Broccoli, green ....:	1,027	941	1,133	1,047
Corn, sweet ....:	4,409	4,462	4,292	4,064
Peas, green ....:	19,988	28,040	17,978	35,590
Spinach ....:	3,038	2,999	4,682	4,328
Other vegetables ....:	1,910	1,911	2,643	2,668
Classification not reported::	3,709	4,062	2,441	3,242
Total ....:	54,141	63,286	52,688	71,774

Compiled from reports of Agricultural Marketing Service.

CPSIA information can be obtained
at www.ICGtesting.com
Printed in the USA
BVHW031152021118
531990BV00020B/1454/P

9 780332 628844